# NORMANDY

# NORMANDY

JACQUELINE WILMES          MARLÈNE ET GÉRARD GSELL

Hermé

# CONTENT

# NORMANDY

## Post Cards and Industries

Five French departments, which in their present boundaries are from the « new map of France destined for use in schools, » date from February 28, 1919. There are six hundred kilometers of coastline, comprising a two-part region, baptized by the Second Empire: Upper Normandy, for the northern departments of the Eure and the Seine-Maritime, and Lower Normandy, to the south, with the Orne, the Calvados and the Manche.

One of the oldest regions of France, a state within the state and born of a formidable alliance between invaders coming from the cold - the Vikings - and the Francs, Normandy produced tough men infinitely richer than the kings of France. Some were even kings of England. Normandy is a land of history and stories, told by abbeys, cathedrals, old neighborhoods which survived the War as well as by half-timbered houses or modest chapels in villages. And the ruins...

Flashing images : Apple trees, fat cows and cuisine rich with cream. Forests and castles. Friendly little cities, which have kept the faded charm from a novel by Maupassant (Ry), from a painting by Boudin (Trouville), Claude Monet (Giverny, Etretat). Beaches along the Pearly Coast (Côte de Nacre), the Floral Coast (Côte Fleurie), where ladies in shapely dresses pose for the Impressionists. White cliffs of the Alabaster Coast (Côte d'Alabâtre) or craggy rocks in the Cotentin. « Marvels » with a capital M : Mont Saint-Michel. Solid gold seaside resorts, which since the romantic years provide a gathering place for the jet set society with impeccable golf courses and flower-laden race tracks.

The Normandy of today shows two faces. One is these pleasant « post cards, » which have attracted artists and tourists for almost five centuries and where each visitor finds what he is looking for.

Around ancient cities with their poetic decor of yesteryear (Le Harve, Rouen, Caen), men have created industrial complexes piece by piece since WW II. They have launched their region into the economic race. They have given themselves the means, by constructing one of the first highway networks in France, the Normandy Freeway and the three bridges across the Seine which complete it. This is the other face of today's Normandy.

# HISTORY OF A DUKEDOM

At the very end of land, the Normandy coasts, as those of Armorique (Brittany), always attracted men in quest of game to hunt. They came from the plains of the Danube and, stopped by the sea, settled in these gentle lands.

The existence of Normandy has been estimated well before the Paleolithic period. Vestiges uncovered by the lowering of the sea during the Quaternary period, the cliffs of the Cotentin and the Anglo-Norman islands (Chausey, for one) bear witness to this fact. The first visible traces of man, found in Calvados in 1828, date back to the late stone age, the end of the Neolithic period, around 3600 years BC.

Somewhat forgotten by tourists, on a small road between Caen and Falaise, in Fontenay-le-Marmion, in the burial grounds of La Hogue and La Hoguette, twelve funeral chambers recount a structured social life and a certain artistic sense.

At the end of the bronze age (1200 - 700), the Seine was already used as a means of transport towards the interior of the continent, for both men and merchandise. It was by this route that, for centuries, the barbarians arrived and dispersed in the Cotentin and the south and settled there. The hordes coming from Belgium took root in the Bocage and the Manche.

## Caesar against Viridorix

When Caesar Augustus arrived, coming by way of the Armorique, those who would be called the Gaulois already occupied the cities named:

Rouen (Rotomagus), Evreus (Mediolanum), Lisieux (Lexoves), Avranche (Avrincates), Caen, Lillebonne (Juliobona), Coutances (Costancia). It was in Bayeux (Augustodurum), that the Roman leader placed his government and his « spearhead » in view of England.

As always in cases of emergency, rival tribes form a united front to fight back at the invader and choose a common leader. They chose Viridorix, an Unelle from what is now the Manche. In 56 BC, the legions of Tiberius Sabinus, heading for England, defeated Viridorix near Carentan.

This marked the beginning of a period which would last more than 800 years and which would give to the future Normandy part of its present-day structures. For their chariots, the Romans took advantage of Gaulois roads, marking them simply with upright stones and thus created a network of roads which follow almost the same routes as our roads today. Vestiges of theaters uncovered in Andelys (Andeleius), in Eu (Augusta), and in Evreux date from this long Roman occupation.

When Christianity was overtly implanted in 260 in Rouen, where Saint-Nicaise founded the first bishopric, the whole of the domains of Neustrie occupied almost the limits of what would become the Dukedom of Normandy (Duché de Normandie) from the X century.

## The Time of Cathedrals

At the beginning of the V century (406), the Germanic tribes infiltrated into Gaul and went as far south as the Loire. It was not the first foreign invasion, but the Francs would solidly settle themselves on these fertile lands of the Il de France and Normandy, and leave their permanent mark upon them. From the Franc epoch, among other things, date Norman terminology in « court » and « city ».

The tribes were pagan, but one of their leaders intelligently adopted the Catholic faith and an already powerful church. Clovis (481 - 511), after having conquered all Gaul, except the Septimanie (Languedoc-Roussillon), overran Normandy in 486. He was baptized in 496 and opened the way for builders of cathedrals.

In Couttance, texts recount the miracle of Saint-Lô, dating from 511 ; others, at Lisieux, date from 538. Encouraged by the Mérovingiens, Saint-Wandrille built an abbey on the Fontanella river (659 and Saint-Ouen founded the diocese of Rouen. In 652 Sainte Austreberthe opened the Pavilly abbey for women. In 654,

Saint Philibert founded Jumièges. Fécamp dates from 660. There was also Saint Marcouf, in the Cotentin. Finally, on Mount Tombe, which was a sacred Druid location, Saint-Aubert, bishop of Avranches, had the first chapel dedicated to Saint-Michel built.

## The Vikings

From the year 800 (the reign of Charlemagne), tough blond men sailing in impressive ships, protected by aggressive prows and rigged with red and blue sails, landed on the coasts of the Manche, spreading terror. They came from the cold Scandinavian regions, armed with heavy swords and seemed to fear neither God nor the devil. People of that time gave them the name « northman » : the Norman.

In 836, the bishop of Coutances fled, taking with him the relics of Saint-Lô, before the Vikings burnt his church. In 841, going up the Seine, they burnt Jumièges and Saint-Wandrille. In 856, a Danish fleet came up the Seine, razed Rouen and destroyed everything from there to Mantes, where they set up a garrison. In 876, the « northman » settled in Rouen. In 900, Coutances was destroyed by a tribe commanded by the leader Rollon.

Miracle of Normandy. As the Francs had done before them, the Vikings settled in the gentle countryside, much easier to live in than their frozen homelands. They found everything they needed there to produce an agriculture they had never before imagined. They especially appreciated water for transport and the sea, to continue their expeditions and ...fishing. These untiring warriors created such fear that the peaceful king of the Francs, Charles III, called « the Simple One », decided to surrender. In 911, at Saint-Clair-sur-Epte, near Gisors, he signed a treaty with the Viking leader Rollon. The treaty conceded the bishoprics of Rouen, Evreux and Lisieux to the Viking in exchange for his promise to convert to Christianity and Christianize his tribes. The first « useful » union in history, he gave Rollon his daughter in marriage. It was a clever strategy as he made the conceded Norman territories into a Dukedom and made Rollon his vassal. Before his destitution, Charles would concede a large part of Lower Normandy (Bayeux, Avranches, Coutances) to Rollon. The promise of Normandy being a vassal to the king of France would endure, however, until Louis XI.

Numerous Norman proper names date from these Scandinavians (Angot, Anquetil, Toutain...) as well as many words used in marine vocabulary. These words are not found in documents which pre-date the arrival of the Vikings.

Rollon was baptized in Rouen in 912. He would launch what would be, for more than a century, the golden age of religious buildings in Normandy. Bishops and monks built or re-built abbeys, cathedrals, Jumièges, Saint-Martin de Bocherville, Bec Hellouin and most of the Roman abbey-churches of which superb vestiges remain.

## When the Norman Reigned over England

At the end of the X century (987), the Vikings were infinitely more powerful than the king, Hugues I Capet, whose kingdom was reduced to the Île de France. In 1027, the newly crowned Robert I, the Magnificent, (Robert the Devil, according to legend) settled in Rouen and obtained French Vexin, which adjoined his domain. Normandy then extended all the way to Pontoise...for several years.

In Falaise, the new duke met the daughter of a leather worker. Their love brought forth a son that same year. The son was named Guillaume (William) and his contemporaries called him « the Bastard » (« le Bâtard ») until his dazzling exploits would make of him Guillaume le Conquérant (William the Conqueror). He would be the first Duke of Normandy to mount the throne of England. In 1047, Guillaume, in turn, allied himself with the king of France, Henri I. He also subdued the barons who were still hostile to Christianity. He settled in Caen, married Mathilde de Flandres and began to subjugate his Angevin neighbors. In 1063, his state was the richest in known Europe. For all of this, the Lord of Normandy did not forget his

Scandinavian roots and his relations with these remarkable seamen formed the basis of important international trade which is still in existence.

He wanted more. Under the pretext that the Anglo-Saxon Harold had chased Edward the Confessor from the throne, Guillaume embarked at Crotoy September 28, 1066, the day of Saint-Michel. On October 14, he confronted Harold II at Hastings, marched on London and, by Christmas, had himself crowned king of England. Normandy became an English province but would remain the favorite land of the duke-kings.

As a sign of jubilation, Guillaume let Jumièges, the cathedral of Evreux and that of Bayeux profit from the wealth acquired in England (and from the revenue of the English crown). For the cathedral of Bayeux he also commissioned a long embroidered fresco : the famous « tapestry ».

His legacy gave rise to serious conflict between his sons, Robert I Courteheuse (Coourtecuisse), the older, and Henri I Beauclerc, the younger. Henri managed to snatch the dukedom of Normandy from his brother after bloody battles at Bayeux and Tinchebray. It is to him that Normandy owes a part of it's fortified castles, notably Nonancourt, Illiers, Verneuil and the fortifications of Pontorson.

## The Passion of the Queen of France

Upon the death of Henri I (1135), his daughter Mathilde inherited the crown. She was married to Geoffroy V « le Bel », called Plantagenêt, count of Anjou and of Maine, who thus became Duke of Normandy (1144). It was a dukedom which extended all the way to the Loire. Crowned when he was seventeen, Henri II, the son of Geoffroy, would enlarge it even more. In 1151, while giving homage to Louis VII, the young duke met the queen of France, the very rich Aliénor of Aquitaine. He was hardly nineteen years old ; she was almost thirty, but her pleasant husband, Louis VII called Le Moine (the monk), gave her little pleasure. This ardent young duke with auburn hair was courageous and cultivated. Born in Le Mans, he spoke French and Latin. Perhaps the immense dukedom which Aliénor possessed had something to do with the attention the young man paid her. She was, however, also beautiful.

On March 21, 1152, the pope declared the king and queen of France divorced. On May 12, a bolt from the blue: Aliénor of Aquitaine remarried to the Duke of Normandy. By this union, the territories of the duke covered almost half of France as it is known today. December 6, 1154, the couple embarked at Barfleur, in weather fit for the judgment of God. On December 19, they were crowned at Westminster. Henri II became the most Norman of the kings of England. He made his beloved dukedom the center of his government and spent more than sixteen years of his reign in his chateaux Petit-Quevilly (Rouen) and Domfront.

The dream of Henri and Aliénor was to see one of their four sons reign over England, Normandy and Aquitaine. Their dream was never to be. Upon the death of Henri, in 1186, his third and only surviving son, Richard, inherited the three crowns of England, Aquitaine and Normandy. Being absent from his kingdom leading the Crusades, the « Cœur de Lion » (Lion-Hearted) was hardly ever in his kingdom until 1196, when he built the crushing fortress of Chateau Gaillard, in Les Andelys. When he died, three years later, Philippe II Auguste, king of France, had already begun to take back the Norman territory: Bray, Eu, Gournay. The cruel Jean Sans Terre was more interested in gaming than defending his continental possessions.

## The Hundred Years War

On March 8, 1204, Chateau Gaillard, which Richard had believed invincible, fell into the hands of Philippe. Rouen surrendered. Normandy became French, but not all Normandy, and not yet definitively. In order to keep his lovely province (plus Anjou, Maine and Touraine), the great grandson of Philippe Auguste, Louis IX - Saint Louis - made an exchange with the king of England against Charente and Auvergne. For this reason the Hundred Years War would start in Normandy. The barons rebelled against a taxation which they judged (already) heavier than that of England. Thus, when Edward III wanted to claim the lands of his ancestors and debarked at Saint-Vaast-la-Hougue on July 12, 1346, it was with the help and complicity of the Norman barons. The Hundred Years War was launched.

Within five weeks, Edward had burned Carentan, then Saint-Lô, Lisieux, Caen, Elbeuf and then went up the Seine all the way to Poissy. The last bastion of resistance, Saint-Valéry-en-Caux surrendered in 1422. Mont-Saint-Michel resisted until 1434.

In the meantime, something had changed during the war. A shepherdess from Domrémy managed to convince the timid Charles VII to fight to regain his kingdom. In 1429, Charles re-captured Orleans. Jeanne, having been taken prisoner, was burned at the stake in Rouen in 1431 without the king defending her in any way. But victory had changed sides. The French re-captured Harfleur, Fécamp, Dieppe, Louviers, Verneuil. On November 10, 1449, Charles VII made a triumphant entry into Rouen. On August 12, 1450, the king bombarded Cherbourg, which surrendered. Normandy had « come home to France. »

## French Normandy

Louis XI, the first king of France to think in terms of unity for the kingdom, created

14

a Normandy Parliament in Rouen. He also gave the city the privilege of a fair, which he took away from Caen, Rouen's rival city. Artists from Tours and Italy embellished the cathedral of Rouen, built the Parliament and the Finance Ministry. From the beginning of the Renaissance, the Valois would continued this work and thus created a true Norman Gothic style which future generations would admire. In August 1517, François I ordered the construction of a new, well-sheltered port at the mouth of the Seine, the Havre-de-Grace. Surely, a bit of Viking blood still runs in the veins of Norman men. These seemingly quiet, land-loving men would show themselves to be daring navigators, venturing forth to discover new worlds at the same time as the Genoese and the Venetians. Norman Huguenots, constituting a majority (except for Dieppe, Saint-Lô, Pont de l'Arche), did not wait for Saint-Barthélémy (1573) to pillage religious buildings (Caen, Cerisy-la-Forêt). The Saint-Barthélémy massacre, perpetrated by Charles X and Catherine de Médicis, was the signal for a brutal civil war which would continue well after the conversion of Henri IV (1593), until the Edit de Nantes (1598).

Once peace was restored, religious leaders undertook to restore the vestiges of their churches and in little more than a century, would build seventeen abbeys or collegiate churches. This was the epoch of chateaux built for pleasure: Balleroy, Beaumesnil, Beaumont, Mandeville-en-Bessin, Carrouges. It was also a time for military constructions, designed to defend the ports (Saint-Vaast La Hougue, Port en Bessin, Granville); the possibility of an English invasion was never excluded.

## From the Empire to the Normandy Invasion

Cherbourg was the last port built after the Revolution. Napoléon inaugurated it in 1811. He could not know that when his body was brought back to France in 1840, it would debark there.

Through the time of kings, an empire, and three republics, Normandy remains. From 1942, it suffered two raids from the Allies at Bruneval and Dieppe which did not go unnoticed by the Germans. The blockhouses which made up the « Atlantic wall » replaced swimmers on the beaches. On June 6, 1944, Montgomery's men began the Liberation by landing on the coast of Normandy. The German garrison of Le Harve would continue to hold fast well after the liberation of Paris, until September 13.

And Normandy began to reconstruct.

1

1. Claude Monet peignit cinquante-six toiles à Giverny.
2. Château-Gaillard, la forteresse de Richard Cœur de Lion.

1. *Claude Monet painted fifty-six canvases at Giverny.*
2. *Chateau-Gaillard, the fortress of Richard the Lion Hearted (Richard Cœur de Lion).*

2 ▶

3

4

5

3. Gisors a conservé maisons et passages du Moyen Âge.
4. Le château de Gisors, place forte des ducs de Normandie.
5. L'église Saint-Denis dans le petit bourg de Lyons-la-Forêt.
6. La hêtraie de Lyons : l'une des plus belles de France.

*3. Gisors has preserved its Middle Age houses and passageways.*
*4. The chateau of Gisors, stronghold of the Dukes of Normandy.*
*5. The St.-Denis church, in the little village of Lyons-la-Forêt.*
*6. The beech grove in Lyons : one of the most beautiful in France.*

7. 185/187 rue Eau-de-Robec à Rouen, une maison du XV<sup>e</sup> siècle.
8. Rouen, dominée par la flèche de la cathédrale.

*7. 185-187 rue Eau-de-Robec, in Rouen, a house from the XV century.*
*8. The cathedral spire towering above Rouen.*

10

9. Dieppe, un port déjà utilisé au VII<sup>e</sup> siècle.
10. La tour du château de Dieppe construite par Richard I<sup>er</sup>.
11. Au Tréport, les falaises de craie de la côte d'Albâtre.
12. À Étretat, l'arche de la Manneporte.

*9. Dieppe, an active port since the VII century.*
*10. The tower of the chateau of Dieppe, built by Richard I.*
*11. Le Tréport, the chalk cliffs of the « Côte d'albâtre » (The Alabaster Coast).*
*12. In Etretat, the Manneporte arch.*

13

13. Fécamp : le château des ducs de Normandie.

13. *Fécamp : the chateau of the Dukes of Normandy*

# THE VALLEY OF THE SEINE,
## a Route to the Sea

Napoleon said of the Seine that it was a natural route towards the sea and one easy to navigate. For centuries it was preferred to roads. It was the Seine which allowed the Vikings to invade Normandy. It also carried the great cathedral builders as well as the first « tourists ».

From the XVIII century, a regular passenger service between Paris and the sea was in place. The journey was slow but fairly comfortable. To travel upstream from Rouen to Paris, fifteen to twenty days of navigation was necessary, varying according to the condition of the state of the water. Passengers were carried on barges pulled by eight or ten « strong horses ». To travel in the other direction, a week was required.

The ancient Roman network of roads, which links Normandy to Brittany, the north, Paris, the Alps and the Mediterranean, has served as a basis for our present roads. The Romans were not great sailors and it was by road that they traveled upstream and sent oysters and shellfish back to Rome. The seafood had been fished from the Channel and packed in ice which had been kept from winter in « snow houses. » Until well into the XIX century, the « tide-chasers » continued to bring fish from the Norman coast to Paris.

Until the time of the railroads, stage coaches followed the banks of the Seine. These made for a rough journey, quicker, but exhausting and dusty. One only has to re-read *Boule de Suif* by Maupassant to imagine these journeys.

In 1841, English workers began construction on the Paris-Le Harve train line. In 1843, the Paris-Rouen section was opened. On March 21, 1847, the completed line was solemnly inaugurated. Six First Class cars brought dignitaries to Le Harve...where the mayor, who put no faith in this dirty mechanical contraption, did not even turn out to welcome them. Seven hours were required to complete this 228 km journey and only 5 hours and 45 minutes when the fast train did not stop at seventeen stations. Today the journey takes hardly more than an hour and a half.

The first trains brought hardy adventurers to Normandy, painters who came to work in Dieppe, Rouen and Etretat. Then came the writers, some of which were of Norman origin. Barbey d'Aureville wrote about Cotentin. Victor Hugo came to Villequier. Flaubert owned a house with blue shutters in Croisset, near Rouen where he was born. It was on the Paris-Le Harve line that Zola set the drama of *La Bête Humaine*. He did not exaggerate the railroad crossings every 4 kilometers, nor the water stops. « Naturalism » (meaning love of nature) became fashionable and was strongly condemned by the Goncourt brothers.

At the beginning of the century, Maurice Leblanc, from Rouen, and creator of the fictional character Arsène Lupin, was as much a sportsman as his fictional gentleman burglar. When he cycled from Etretat to Paris along the right bank of the Seine (Rt. D.982), he discovered the great abbeys, where his fictional Lupin would commit his burglaries. Even today, following the banks of the Seine is still the prettiest route to reach Normandy.

## The Seine in the Eure Department

The Seine enters Normandy in the department of the Eure. Flanked by countryside and spectacular cliffs, the charm of this valley has not yet been marred by housing projects or industrial parks. It was on the Seine that the first dukes of Normandy built their fortresses, which defended their dukedom against neighboring France. It was also on the Seine that

the last battles of August, 1944, were fought, just before the liberation of Paris. Vernon and Les Andelys, Allied spearheads, have recovered from these battles in different ways.

Dating from the time Vernon was on the defensive, remain four towers from the chateau des Tourelles, which are as old as the Collégiale. The old city, where houses which survived the War have been restored, has nothing to do with the sad streets where Zola's *Thérèse Raquin* spent long boring hours in her sad shop, selling threads and buttons. A sensible peripheral urbanization and secondary residences assure, on week-ends, a permanent liveliness among the half timbered-houses and the very lovely Collégiale Notre-Dame. The Collégiale was founded by Guillaume de Vernon in 1160. The Office of Tourism, housed in its corbelled bourgeois dwelling from the XV century, is not to be missed in the Rue Potard. The Museum Poulain, half-timbered also shows the elegance of private Norman town houses from the XVII to the XVIII century. This museum is a curiosity with its collection of animal art of the highest quality. It contains sculptures by Pompon, Bugatti, paintings by Rosa Bonheur, Vuillard, Money as well as archeological collections which retrace the history of Vernon from the Neolithic period.

At 2 km, in the forest, the chateau of Bizy rises among the trees in a lovely French-style park, complete with waterfalls. Built for the Marchal-Duke of Belle-Isle, grandson of Fouquet, its construction is as elegant as that of Vaux-le-Vicomte with pools decorated with sea horses and stables copied from those of Versailles. The rooms, richly decorated and furnished, somewhat recalling Pompadour, give an idea of its past splendor.

At Les Andelys (two cities in one, thus its plural name), a number of beautiful dwellings, such as Le Grand Cerf, frequented by Victor Hugo and Walter Scott were destroyed. History tells us that it was at Grand Andeley that the queen Clotilde converted her husband, Clovis, the head of the Francs. In gratitude, she founded a monastery and the Clotilde fountain bears witness to the miracle of this conversion. Behind the Museum Nicolas Poussin, the church of Notre-Dame dates from the XIII century. The portal and the sculptured gallery, reworked during the Renaissance, are beautiful examples of flamboyant gothic. At the end of the Avenue de la République, on the banks of the Seine, the Petit Andely was somewhat important during the Galo-Roman period (Andelius). Augustus Caesar organized games in the theater, which excavations in the neighboring village, Noyers, have brought to light. The parish church Saint-Sauveur has retained the purity of its high vault and pointed arches, which give it true grandeur. Several half-timbered houses surround the church and on the quays a part of the Middle Age roadbed has been brought to light.

Five minutes from there, following the Rue Richard Cœur de Lion, Chateau-Gaillard overlooks a bend in the Seine. Upon his return from the Crusades, Richard of England had this formidable fortress built in two years (1196-1197). The walls of the dungeon measure five meters thick. It took Philippe Auguste eight months of siege and a mortal assault to achieve his victory (March 8, 1204) and return Normandy back to France. From the ramparts one has the same view of the Seine that the Cœur de Lion (the Lion Hearted) had eight centuries ago.

## Rouen, History of a Capital

The Seine enters the department of Seine Maritime at Criquebœuf, at the port of Rouen, in the suburbs. The history of this port has been linked to that of Normandy since the time it was Gaul. The Vikings, as was their habit, razed the city (841), then reconstructed it and settled in. They maintained a slave market where they sold Flemish and Irishmen. After his treaty with Charles III, Rollon had himself baptized in 912, showing how important the city was for him. Guillaume le Conquérant (William the Conqueror) and Henri II of England had the heads of their continental governments there. Louis XI conferred the status of regional capital to Rouen, a status which it has kept against all odds. The city, in the form we know it, began on the right bank of the Seine during the time of William the Conqueror.

## Rouen 2000

In the XVIII century, a circular boulevard was built on the former fortifications. This was the beginning of the industrial era in France, and Rouen played its role. It was called the French Manchester. To hold its own with Lyon in manufacturing high quality fabrics, Rouen produced, notably, a cotton velvet called rouennerie. Rouen already had a modern port in 1939.

The Battle of Normandy respected most of the historic city but practically destroyed the port and the merchant docks, which the artists Corot and Pissaro had painted. From 1945, the port of Rouen rekindled its economic activity. In 1998, it was the largest port in Europe for the exportation of grains, flours, and fertilizer as well as the most important port for exportation to Africa, the Indian Ocean and the Antilles.

During the 1960s, the Regional Counsel intelligently implanted modern structures on the left bank, notably the Police Prefecture and an Administration Center. New high-rise housing projects surrounded these. Rouen 2000, « Greater Rouen » consists of 400,000 inhabitants only 150,000 of which live in Old Rouen. But the heart of the city remains, in spite of everything. The city is like a museum, but remains lively, young and active, thanks perhaps to the new blood of modern Rouen.

## ...and the eternal Rouen

A thousand half-timbered houses, scrupulously restored, shops, bistros, and 6 km of a walk through history are all a part of the city : Rue Saint-Romain, behind the cathedral, Rue Eau de Robec, whose corbelled houses are rare specimens since Frrançois I forbade their construction in the name of modernity in 1520. Between the cathedral and the Old Market square, one finds the pedestrian street of the Gros Horloge (Big Clock), the most frequented by young people. Shops and snack bars are overlooked by the Renaissance belfry and arch which supports the famous seven-day Gros Horloge, the pride of Rouen since the XIV century.

By chance, in one of the old streets, one may come across monuments which make this city an open-air museum, where pure gothic style is mixed with original Roman construction. For example, Saint-Maclou, whose simple building dates from the earliest times of Christianity, and whose atrium with houses on wooden pillars shelter what is left of leper-houses. There is Saint-Ouen, a breathtaking gothic abbey-church, began in 1318. The fabulous gothic Palais de Justice (Courthouse) was where Louis XI and François I held their Courts of Justice. The Salle des Séances (Courtroom) has preserved its ceiling of sculpted squares intact.

The Place du Vieux Marché, where Jeanne d'Arc was burned is a must. In the church of 1970, one can see 500 square meters of sparkling stained glass windows, taken down and kept in a safe place in 1939. Renaissance woodwork gives some indication of what the Eglise Saint Vincent must have been like before it was destroyed during the war. In the market, held six days a week, ducks, cheese and cold regional meats all attract lovers of fine food.

In the heart of Old Rouen stands the breathtaking Cathedral Notre-Dame, began under the Plantagenêt (XII century). It is so impressive that Monet painted it in thirty versions. The lantern tower, whose columns rise up to 50 meters, has a history. Its spire, built in 1544, lasted until a lightning bolt destroyed it in 1822. The first architect called in suggested a spire in wrought iron, a revolutionary material which had only just begun to be used in industrial constructions. This was proclaimed a scandal! It took almost sixty years (1881) for the spire which now dominates the city to be finally finished. Viollet-le-Duc, jealous, called the spire a « pyramid of junk meta ».

Almost everyone in Rouen passes sometime during the day through Cathedral Square. It is surrounded by restaurants and terraces which are always full when the weather is fine. Facing the St-Jean and St-Etienne portals (XII century), stands an exquisite Renaissance house, the former Bureau des Finances (1510) (Finance Ministry) which now houses the Office of Tourism. Alas, a Convention Center made of pure concrete, built in 1970 and which public officials have since dreamed of tearing down, constitutes the only blemish in these poetic surroundings.

The Museum of Fine Arts is inevitable for the visitor. In this museum next to works by Caravage hang canvases by the great Dutch landscape painters, works by Velasquez as well as paintings by Delacroix, Géricault, Poussin, Millet, Boudin, Corot, Pissaro... all of which speak of another age.

## The Abbey Route

In the last bends of the Seine, between the river and the forests, some of the most spectacular Norman abbeys have preserved their incomparable atmosphere.

Leaving Rouen, the route D 982 crosses the forest of Roumare before arriving in Saint-Martin de Boscherville, the first stone of which was laid in 1050 by a chamberlain of William the Conqueror. The resurrection of Medieval buildings (the capitals are in the Museum of Rouen) owes a debt to the good will of volunteers, directing the work of unemployed youth. The lantern tower and a part of the old cloisters are usually restored to their original state. Italian style gardens and flower beds of white roses give them a soul. In the simple village, where everyone is proud of their abbey, the parish church of Saint-George has regained its original purity.

From the village of Duclair, capital of Norman ducks (a special duck market takes place on Tuesdays), one of the last six ferries on the Seine travels to Jumièges and its abbey. The Potemkin facades of the abbey project sculpted stone 43 meters into the sky. Two towers, a destroyed nave, a small tower, are all that remain of Notre-Dame. For Saint-Pierre there remains a porch and several beams and a giant pile of rubble and stone, still imprinted with peace. Agnès Sorel, the « dame de Beauté » (lady of beauty), mistress of Charles VII, stopped there with him on their way to Rouen. She was so moved by this atmosphere that she wanted to be buried there.

The access to the Brotonne bridge, which has opened up this bend in the Seine since 1977, brings a great deal of activity to Saint-Wandrille during the season. The abbey and the village were once called Fontanelle, like the stream near which Wandrille, baron of the King Dagobert, had the original basilica built. A superb Roman ruin, Saint Pierre and the usual convent buildings, were all but forgotten since the French Revolution. Georgette Leblanc, sister of the author, rented the cloister with her lover Maurice Maeterlinck at the beginning of the century because her brother, riding by there on his bicycle, thought this spot held a romanticism worthy of Walter Scott. Many celebrities of the period spent time here and the fictitious Arsène Lupin lived out several of his adventures here. Reread « La Comtesse de Cagliostro ».

Since 1931, Benedictine monks have been settled in the abbey. They have been trying to restore, in an architectural sense, the cloister and the convent buildings. They have created an impressive church in a structure from the XIII century, transporting stones one by one. They celebrate mass with Gregorian chants.

## Victor Hugo's House

In Caudebec en Caux, the puffins, coming down from Le Harvre, give way to the « margats » coming up to Rouen. These are pilots which have followed the Seine for more than a century. However, stopped by the dams, the tidal bore, this worrying menace of the depths coming in from the sea, once watched as a family outing, is now no more than a big wave and inspires fear in no one. The Naval Museum of the Seine perpetuates the legend.

In Villequier, on September 14, 1843, the bodies of Léopoldine, favorite daughter of Victor Hugo, and her young husband Charles Vacquerie were brought into a large bourgeois house of the last century, the most imposing in the village. They had hardly been married six months. The Vacquerie house is now the lovely Museum Hugo. Above Caudebecq, at the foot of the church Saint-Martin, which Henri IV called « the most beautiful chapel in the kingdom, » lies the poetic little cemetery where the young couple are buried. It is always full of roses and heather, as Victor Hugo would have wanted.

# Le Havre : the Age of Grand Voyages

For more than five centuries the port desired by François I at the back of the mouth of the Seine was called Harvre de Grâce. Around 1815, Le Harve specialized in the transport of cotton, coal and minerals, as well as passengers. In 1850, the Benjamin Franklin made the Paris-New York crossing in fourteen days.

The prestigious Compagnie Générale Transatlantique, the « Transat », built legendary steamships: the Paris, the Île de France, and in 1935, the Normandie, called « the most beautiful steamship in the world ». The Normandie surpassed the Cunard line and received the « Blue Ribbon » for the fastest crossing from Le Harve to New York.

In 1945, Le Harve was the « most seriously damaged port in Europe ». One hundred and fifty-six bombings, 11,000 tons of bombs, 19,650 buildings shattered, it was a port destroyed by the Germans. It took two years to clear away the ruins.

The architect Auguste Perret, the « concrete magician » who directed its reconstruction, conceived an ambitious plan from which would emerge a new city with wide avenues and giant squares (the Town Hall square remains the largest in Europe). The city would be studded with solid monuments such as the tower of the Town Hall (72 meters high), the monumental Church Saint Joseph, the André Malraux Museum of Fine Arts. It was a city too big to appear alive, in spite of the creation of a University in 1986 to attract young people.

The reconstructed port managed to keep its mysterious atmosphere until the 1970s, an atmosphere found in the famous film *Quai des Brumes*. It was a place where freight departed for distant destinations, where tired heroes of more adventurous times lingered about. It included a hangar for cotton more than 2 kilometers long; a port for wood, or where automobiles were dwarfed between blocks of mahogany higher than trucks; scales which were razed to let trailers pass.

Le Harve has regained its place as the largest commercial port in France and the fifth largest in Europe. A visit around the port by boat, La Salamandre, gives an idea of its gigantic dimensions. Cargo ships have become container carriers, large ferries for England and Irland have replaced the steamships and transported more than a million passengers in 1997. Near the mouth of the Seine, a gigantic industrial complex has been built-over 10,000 hectares, which extends to Harfleur and the banks of the Seine all the way past Tancarville. This complex is reached by a bridge worthy of its name: the Normandy bridge (1995), the longest in the world, 2141 meters in length.

From its history, Le Harve has kept its Notre Dame cathedral, in the Saint-François neighborhood, the district of the whalers, several houses from the XVIII century, the «hotel Brocques» and the church built by Jérôme Ballarmato. In a lovely shipbuilder's home, near the ferry station, the Museum of Old Harve recounts the saga of the old port.

Overlooked by the Sainte-Adresse hill, the northern beach of Le Harve owes its celebrity to the director of the Figaro, Alphonse Karr. Settled in Etretat, Karr was intrigued by this fishing port and built one of the first villas there in 1840. Eugène Boudin exhibited his first canvases in the small book shop in the center of town and the Société des Régates is the largest French nautical club. In 1914-1918, Albert I of Belgium and his government were housed here.

The splendors of the Belle Époque remain in several villas (la Villa Maritime). The chic hotels have now become apartments and a lot of construction has taken place higher up in the hills. However, Sainte-Adresse, a residential area as well as a seaside resort, with its shops and bistros, remains a place for the population of Le Harve to have an outing. And for those who are fond of fun boards, they may practice their sport all year round; adepts of the sport judge this location to be as good as Biarritz, when there is a nice wind.

15

14. Le Pont de Normandie, 2 141 mètres de long, a été inauguré en 1995.
15. Chaumières et pommiers : le Marais Vernier.
16. Le Marais Vernier a été construit par les Hollandais.

*14. The Normandy Bridge (Pont de Normandie), inaugurated in 1995, 2141 meters long.*
*15. Thatched roof cottages and apple trees : Marais Vernier.*
*16. The Dutch built Marais Vernier.*

◀ 14

16

17. Le Vieux Bassin à Honfleur, un port du XVII<sup>e</sup> siècle.
*17. Le Vieux Bassin (The Old Dock), in Honfleur, a port since the XVII century.*

19

20

18. Une pêche très active, quai de la Touque, à Trouville.

◄ 18    *18. A very active fishing port, quay de la Touque, in Trouville.*

19. « Les planches » de Deauville : le rendez-vous du matin.
20. Deauville a bien conservé son style normand
21. La plage de Cabourg, toujours telle que la peignit Prinet.
22. Autour d'Arromanches, la côte de Nacre.

*19. « Les planches » (The Boardwalk) of Deauville : the place to meet in the morning.*
*20. Deauville has preserved its Normandy style.*
*21. The beach at Cabourg, still just like Prinet painted it.*
*22. Around Arromanches, the « Côte de nacre » (The Pearly Coast).*

22 ▶

23

23. L'abbaye bénédictine du Bec-Hellouin a été reconstruite en 1948.
24. Le village de Bec-Hellouin a survécu à tous les pillages.
25. La tour Saint-Nicolas, vestige du XVᵉ siècle.

*23. The Abbey of Bec Hellouin, reconstructed in 1948.*
*24. The village of Bec Hellouin managed to survive all the plundering of the past.*
*25. The Saint-Nicolas Tower, a vestige of the XV century.*

24

25

26. Conches-en-Ouche, une petite ville chargée d'histoire.
27. Les maisons-manoir du Pays d'Ouche.

*26. Conches-en-Ouche, a small city full of history.*
*27. Manor houses in the Pays d'Ouche.*

28. La cathédrale d'Évreux, l'une des plus belles de Normandie.
*28. The Evreux cathedral, one of the most beautiful in Normandy.*

# DEPARTMENT OF SEINE MARITIME

## The Alabaster Coast

From Le Harve to Dieppe, the sea has roughly dug into the chalk which accounts for the cliffs being called the « Alabaster Coast ». These are strange cliffs, torn with valleys-their whiteness, added to the Normandy sky, produces a transparency in every season which was so appreciated by the impressionists.

In Etretat, Corot, Coubet, Pissaro, Claude Monet, Delacroix, the Dutch painter Jongkind, in all kinds of light, set about painting the high cliff of Aval and the Manneporte arch which closes the beach. In 1833, Alphonse Karr, fascinated by the place, settled there. He encouraged the building of roads towards Fécamp, Le Harve and the railroad to Paris (1893). Flaubert, coming from Croisset, Offenbach, in the Orphée villa, and Maupassant, who lived at La Guillette, were all together here during the high season. For a story with the fictional burglar Arsène Lupin, Maurice Leblanc imagined that the immense Aiguille (70 meters) opposite the Manneporte, was « hollow ». If the Aiguille was smoking in the evening, it was a sign that the « gentleman-burglar » was back.

Etretat has changed very little. For sure, in the creek of the Petit Port, sailing dinghies have replaced fishing boats. A public golf course runs up the Aval Cliff.

A good number of néo-Norman chalets have been built in the area. But at sunset, the « Vieux Galets » (the regulars) still climb the Falaise d'Amont all the way to the little church of the fishermen, for a spectacular view over the Manneporte. The old market (les Halles), reconstructed, house well stocked boutiques.

Hidden among the trees, the « Clos Lupin » paid for by Leblanc with his royalties, is still there, like La Guillette, la villa Orphée and many others. There are still enough superb and kitsch « chalets » in Etretat for it to have kept its special atmosphere.

## Fécamp: New Lands

The tiny Rue de Valmont must have used a measuring tape to dig the cliff 126 meters high, which encloses Fécamp. Legend has it that the trunk of a fig tree containing an ampoule of Christ's blood was at the origin of the city's founding. The annual pilgrimage to the relic (in June) proves that the faithful still believe in the legend.

The Vikings were attracted to such a sheltered port and, in 928, Guillaume Longue Epée built the fortified chateau. Impressive vestiges of the fort still overlook the city. In 1521, a ship builder, Nicolas Selles, sent a ship towards the northern seas. His return with a load of codfish launched the fishing industry which made Fécamp the capital of the New Lands. The last of the great fishing boats came back to port in 1987, but the Musée des Terre-Neuvas (The Museum of New Lands) has stored up the touching souvenirs of the difficult life at sea.

Starting at dawn with the fish market, the quay de la Vicomté and the quay Berigny become lively. Later on the boutiques in old Fécamp begin to stir, especially in the Hallette Square, Rue Arquaise, Rue Huet at the foot of the Sainte-Trinité. Built by the great architect monk Guillaume de Volpiano (1003), this basilica remains the largest classic cathedral after Notre-Dame in Paris (127 meters vs. 130).

A Fécamp tradition, the liquor Bénédictine, was invented by a monk by the name of Vincelli, who, in 1510, concocted this « elixir of good health » using herbs and spices. Vincelli's recipe was lost during the French Revolution. In 1863, a merchant named Alexandre Le Grand (his true name) reproduced it and after making it world famous, constructed the astonishing Palais de la Bénédictine. The giant copper vats of the distillery remind one of the time when « industrial processes » were carried out by artisans.

An enigma, Guy de Maupassant, who swore that he was born in the chateau of the Marquis de Miromesnil, near Tourville-sur-Arques, was brought into the world in Fécamp in 1850. The reality is that the Maison Tellier, the funny story of an amiable brothel, is set in Fécamp...but where?

The small departmental road, which follows the coast from Fécamp to Dieppe, goes through villages and minuscule seaside resorts, squeezed in even the smallest of valleys. These are charming stops, somewhat forgotten by time. Among them are Senneville and the Petites Dalles. Two kilometers from there the elegant pink chateau hotel of Sassetot-le-Mauconduit had the Empress Elisabeth of Austria-Sissi-for a guest during the summer of 1875. Saint-Valéry en Caux is kept lively by its pretty marina.

## Dieppe, the Ivory Port

The shortest route from Paris to the sea is the road to Dieppe (D91115). For this reason Dieppe is the oldest seaside resort in France. The historian, Pierre de l'Estoile, recounted that Henri III came « came to bathe in the sea near Dieppe, to cure the itch ». In 1780, the first regular passenger line to England brought British « bathers ». During the Empire (1806) the robust Mme de Boignes had a little coach outfitted with curtains to ride to the sea. In 1820 the crazy Duchess of Berry, daughter-in-law of Charles X, arrived on the scene. A casino and a race track were opened. Isabey painted « Storm over Dieppe » with life guards wearing top hats. Louis-Philippe stayed in the nearby Tréport. Napoléon III followed, after Alexandre Dumas, the duke de Morny, Delacroix and Oscar Wilde. Dieppe was established.

The Boulevard du Maréchal Foch follows the beach which is always edged with flower beds and lawns. This is where Dieppe lives all year, between the casino and the ports. The movement of the ferries awakens the old streets behind the Quay Henri IV. Near there, the fish market, the arrival of fishermen as well as banana boats in the commercial port make this a lively and amusing place. In the recently enlarged marina, French and English crews maintain the typical atmosphere of sailing ports. Near the casino, the tower of the enormous chateau of Richard I, houses a unique collection of objects in ivory. These humble souvenirs were made by seamen and master carvers and remind us of the time when artists from Dieppe worked African ivory. Opposite the port, in Pollet, the ex-neighborhood of fishermen, the stairs lead to Notre-Dame de Bon Secours, for a panorama of the bay and Dieppe.

## From Eu to Le Tréport

Separated by four kilometers on the Bresle, the little city and the seaside resort of the Restauration hardly make up more than one city. They have a common history, that of the Count of Eu, who began their construction in 996. The Conqueror married Mathilde of Flanders in the chateau of Eu. Inherited by Louis-Philippe, it became his favorite residence. It was in this way that the king launched Le Tréport. Sold to the city in 1954 by the Orléans family, this beautiful residence decorated by a bourgeois-king, has preserved the grand green and gold Bragance salon intact. This is where Mlle de Montpensier received guests. Her bedroom is also intact. An astounding

library of 10,000 books and an exposition of crystal from the Bresle valley are also on display. In the coolness of the evening, after visiting the Terrasses of Le Tréport, it makes a good change to visit Eu and the calm of its winding old streets around the Saint-Laurent Church.

## The Regions of Caux and Bray

Between Saint-Valery and Yvetot, the region of Caux was already the breadbasket of Normandy in the XVI century. Quiet country roads cross fields which seem not to have changed in the last hundred years, with the exception of several television antennas. One goes through prairies, wheat fields and villages gathered around small churches. Some of the villages are historic (Valliquerville, near Yvetot, Mesnil Geoffroy). Sometimes one can see half-timbered manor houses and clos-masures, these long farms built in a square around an interior court and surrounded by moats, which, here, are high embankments planted with elm trees. There are exceptional dovecotes, the most impressive of which is that of the manor of Auffray. Yvetot is still the largest market in the Caux region, and this since the XIV century. The September and October fairs have kept the same atmosphere as in past times. The Museum of the Caux Region is a must, where pure Norman interiors have been reconstructed.

Apple trees bend under the weight of fruit, which the cows love. It is said that thanks to the apples the cream has the special «taste of violets» which Chateaubriand seemed to find.

We are now in the Bray region, which follows the length of the Béthune. Here we find forests (Eawy forest, Eu forest), water, houses with red walls : it's the land of Neufchatel, a cheese which was already being made in the XI century. The cheese is molded into six shapes, including a heart shape which is used for celebrations. Over half of the Neufchatel cheese is still made in local dairies. One can see in the Museum of Neufchatel Arts and Traditions that the art of cheese making has not changed much over the years. This fact is proven by the cheese fairs, held in April and November. These occasions are always a good pretext for tasting (and buying). It was in Gournay-en-Bray that the cheese called « Petit Swisse » was invented, around 1850. Some say that it was the recipe of a farm girl, others say it was from a cheese maker. Whatever the origin, the little round cheese created the first industry in the region.

Also in Bray, ancient ruins punctuate the peaceful roads. In the Hellet forest, between Neufchâtel and Arques, there are no less than five charming villages with Romanesque or Gothic churches. In Gournay, the sober Saint-Hildevert Church is an example. In Bouchevilliers, the manor and the church, curiously decorated with squares of stone and brick, date from the XVI century.

## Emma Bovary

In Ry, one can talk to everyone about Mme Bovary. It was in this hamlet that Flaubert set Yonville. It is where the young woman who served as his model, Dellphine Coudurier, lived. The Romanesque belfry of the church and the carved oak porch knew the real Bovary, wife of an authentic Dr. Delamare. In the main street, the Homais pharmacy and the Auberge du Lion d'Or (Golden Lion Inn), where she had meetings with Rodolphe are indicated. And, of course, the most beautiful house in the region belonged to the notary. Si non e vero....

## THE EURE
## The Norman Vexin

At the very door of the Ile de France, between the Eure and the Epte, the very old villages of Norman Vexin feel they belong more to the Île de France than to Normandy. Such is the case with Gisors, which is less than 2 kilometers from the Oise (French Vexin) to which its history is tied.

A friendly provincial village during the week, Gisors comes alive on the weekend when residents of the very Medieval neighboring villages arrive. Built on the Epte to defend the access to Normandy, the chateau dates from 1097. Its enormous dungeon can be seen from far away. From the chateau gardens, one has a view overlooking the gem of Gisors, its Saint-Gervais-Saint-Protais church, which was begun at the beginning of the XII century.

It was the train from Gisors to Vernon which brought Claude Monet, his mistress, Alice Hoschedé, and their eight children to Giverny in the summer of 1883. Monet was forty-three years old and had more debts than success. He was enthusiastic about the village and discovered, at the end of the Roy Road, a vast residence where he painted his most famous canvases. He bought the house and the adjacent land, made deviation in a branch of the Epte to create a Japanese pond, thus creating the famous pond of the « water lilies ». A great number of painters and intellectuals would spend time in this pink house with its green shutters : Pissar, Berthe Morisot, Signac, Bonnard, and also Paul Valéry, Gallimard, George Clémenceau and even Sacha Guitry and the very young Yvonne Printemps.

From April to October, tourists flock to Giverny, which has changed very little since Monet lived there. A bistro now occupies the Baudy house, where the painters stayed. In the springtime, the gardens bloom with colors he painted so well. The home has kept its rare collection of Japanese etchings. Magazines for home decoration continue to photograph the kitchen with its Delft blue tiles and the yellow dining room which Money liked. In time, American painters came to paint on the banks of the Epte : Miller, Robinson, John Sargent, Frederick Frieseke. Several works as well as other expositions are on display in the newly opened Museum of American Art.

On the left bank of the Seine, very popular at week-ends, towns whose history goes back to the first Norman dukes have kept their old neighborhoods and their noble ruins. Verneuil-sur-Avre, as Vernon and Les Andelys, was built to guard the Normandy road. Ivry-la-Bataille is where Henry IV made his famous declaration, « rally round my white plume ». A must to see is the majestic abbey church in Ecouis.

## The Lyons Forest

In the north of the Eure, adjoining the Seine Maritime, the Lyons Forest is one of the largest and oldest beech groves in France : 11,000 hectares of thicket and clusters of tall trees, looked after by the monks of the Mortemer Abbey. One of the oldest trees the Bunodière Beech, 41 meters tall, would have been standing during the French Revolution of 1789.

A walk through the Lyons is like a discovery voyage where one finds villages and Medieval vestiges in the middle of clusters of trees. Lyons-la-Forest, a village classified as an historic monument and an old legendary city, was founded on the spot where once stood one of the chateaux of Henri I of England. The half-timbered houses (rue du Bout-de-Bas) remind us that we are in Normandy. The town hall is the former home of the mounted constabulary of the XVIII century, the school is located on the ruins of the Benedictine Convent (XVI century) and the pretty market dates from the XVII century. Inspired by the peacefulness of the area, Maurice Ravel had a neo-Norman villa built here (1917) where he composed some of his most striking work. In the Church of Saint-Denis, large wooden statues from the XVI century, primitive and moving, complete this voyage into the past.

If this decor seems familiar, it is only natural. It was here that Jean Renoir and Claude

Chabrol filmed their version of *Madame Bovary*, and in addition, Emma recognized her lover here.

Without leaving the forest, look for the Mortemer Abbey, in Lisors. The park with its three ponds frames the vestiges of a Cistercian Abbey and convent buildings from the XVII century. It is said that the ghost of Queen Mathilde roams this place on the nights of the full moon. One can visit the beautiful museum of monastic life and see the monks' cells which are still furnished.

## Evreux, the Yellow City

Evreux, the administrative capital for the Eure department, is less that 100 kilometers from Paris and is hardly further from the sea (120 kilometers). Burned and destroyed a hundred times since the V century and even in 1944, this pretty city has preserved its vestiges and has carefully put them on display along with several lovely bourgeois homes whose warm color comes from sand from the Seine.

In Town Hall Square (Place de l'Hotel de Ville) the Beffroy, called Tour de l'Horloge, reigns over all the business streets. The flower-laden Avenue Robert-de-Flocques is a favorite strolling place for the residents of Evreux. It follows the Galo-Roman ramparts and leads to Notre-Dame cathedral. The astonishing lantern tower, topped with its «silver bell» was already in place during the time of Louis XI. This « silver » dome is actually made of lead, but it has its legend. In 1475, a young plumber by the name of Hugolin agreed to cover the wooden steeple for free, on condition that his old boss, Pierre, would grant him the hand of his daughter. Alas, when he was putting the last sheet of lead in place, Hugolin fell to his death. Next to the cathedral stands the former Episcopal Palace, constructed on the Galo-Roman wall from the III century. The rampart is included in the museum, along with Paleolithic collections and a remarkable collection of earthenware and canvases by Boudin, Géricault...

The Saint Taurin church is visited for the tomb of the saint, chiseled like an Italian jewel and dripping with gold. This also has its legend. Saint Taurin, who founded the Abbey church in the IV century, was the personal enemy of Satan, who would destroy the walls at night. This continued until the night when Taurin caught the devil by the horns and shook him so hard that one of the horns came off and remained in his hands. The devil's horn disappeared during the Revolution and, to believe the legend, there remain only accounts of the incident from the time in which it took place. But the tomb is guarded...by three demons. A pleasant walk in the evening would include the public gardens and its rose garden, built to keep the very old Cloister of the Capucines (XVII century) alive. Only the sculpted wall of the cloister remain.

Since the Middle Ages, Evreux has been the largest agricultural market of the region. The Saturday market and the October and December 6 fairs are worth a visit.

# The Ouche Region

Between Eure and Calvados, the Ouches region is a lovely region for outings. The atmosphere is perhaps a bit darker than that which is found in the novels of Jean de La Varende whose hero *Nez de cuir* lived here. Perched on a small hill (144 meters), Conches is the « capital » of Ouche. This city has paid heavily for every battle since the Hundred Years War. In its history, there have been many beautiful homes with wooden panels. The only church having survived in the four parishes which divide Conches is Sainte-Foy, whose Renaissance stained glass windows make up a dazzling color composition. The Norman Country Museum displays old tools and everyday objects used in a not-so-distant farm life.

From Conches to Bernay, the prettiest road (D.140) runs through the Valley of the Charentonne, sprinkled with villages and chateaux. The most precious, without a doubt, is Beaumesnil. The wide moats enclose an immense and breathtaking Baroque construction of bricks and stones, surrounded by flower beds in the French style. Built in 1633, the chateau houses a unique museum of bookbinding. The treasure of Bernay is its Abbey church, one of the most spectacular in Normandy. The interior decoration, chiseled with friezes and interlacing, reminds one of illuminated manuscripts of the Middle Ages. In checkerboard design of bricks and stones, the abbey residence (XVI century) owes its collections to the enthusiasm of its curators. Rare earthenware from Rouen, Norman furniture, Norman, English and Dutch canvases and paintings make it a charming voyage into the past. In the Sainte-Croix Church, precious pieces of religious art from Bec-Hellouin can be seen.

Crossing the Neubourg plateau, one can discover Harcourt in the midst of clusters of trees. It is the perfect decor for this austere Medieval chateau. Harcourt has preserved its draw bridge and eight of the twelve original towers of its wall. Renovated, the Louis XIII paneling of the large rooms has given the salons back their warm elegance of yesteryear. For those interested, the century-old collections in the arboretum make up the second largest in France.

Nearby, the chateau of Champ de Bataille speaks of another epoch. A green lawn makes a fitting setting for the long and elegant brick structure whose colors have softened with time. The interior rooms are superbly furnished.

## The History of Bec Hellouin

Consisting of several low Norman houses, two antique shops and three small café terraces, the village of Bec Hellouin, on the banks of the Risle, is a destination of pure happiness, provided one is careful not to come on long weekends. At the end off its park, the abbey has stood the test of time. In 1034, the Knight Hellouin and nine companions, renouncing the world and its pleasures, created a religious community with austere rules. In 1045, an Italian monk by the name of Lenfranc, began construction of a monastery. His work lasted 48 years.

Under the reign of Louis XIII, Guillaume de la Trembllaye, the great building master of the Congregation and a fine architect, had the abbey church, the cloister and the infirmary built.

During the Revolution, the convent buildings were pillaged, the bells were melted down and the silver and furniture all sold. The inestimable incunabula of the library were pillaged. The disaster happened under the Empire, when the army used the-ruins to house their horses. It took the intervention of Pierre Mendès-France to get the army to leave Bec-Hellouin. The first new mass to be celebrated there was in September 1948. Today, the white robes of a Benedictine sometimes is seen going through the park. The white Saint-Nicolas tower, a vestige of the abbey from the XV century, is reflected in the waters of the pond. Perfect peace now reigns over this place.

Coming back to the Risle by the small rural roads, the villages one passes through have something different about them. Around simple little Romanesque churches, the old cemeteries are shaded by yew trees, thought to purify the air during the Middle Ages. One chances upon Bouquetot, Bourg-Achard, Monfort-sur-Risle, Bourgtherould, on the edge of the large forest of Brotonnes. The Ecomuseum of the Basse-Seine offers maps and guided tours, for journeys into the past. For example, the Chateau de Robert-le-Diable houses the only Viking museum.

## Henri IV's Apple Trees

On the banks of the Risle, Pont Audemer was baptized the « Norman Venice. » This is a bit excessive, but the various tributaries of the Risle, edged with poetic Norman homes and terraces, give the place a particular charm.

A pretty bridge over the Risle leads to the Marais Vernier (in the Eure-not to be confused with the Marais of the Calvados). Here one is plunged in the Normandy of another era. Green prairies, apple trees, beige colored cows, low roofed wooden and cob cottages, little old churches from the XII century, nothing is missing, neither a House of Apples with it's cider press not a forge. It was Henri IV who had the idea to bring in the Dutch, masters in the matter, to dry up 5000 hectares of mire. The Digue des Hollandias (The Dutch Dike) is still there. Centuries of care and 35 kilometers of canals managed this miracle.

To the north of the Marais Vernier, the Tancarville Bridge (609 meters) was the first constructed after the War (1959) and was the longest in Europe for a long time.

29

29. Les maisons à pans de bois du Pays d'Auge.

*29. Houses with exterior beams in the Pays d'Auge.*

30. Le château Renaissance de Saint-Germain-du-Livet.
31. Sur la route des fromages, le manoir de Bellou.
32. Un des colombiers (XVe siècle) du château de Crèvecœur.

*30. The Renaissance Chateau of St.-Germain-du-Livet.*
*31. On the cheese route, the Manor of Bellou.*
*32. One of the dovecotes (XV century) of the Crèvecœur chateau.*

31

32

33

33. La basilique Sainte-Thérèse à Lisieux (1929).
34. Vimoutiers, capitale du camembert.
35. Au Pays d'Auge, les pommiers de « la Route du Cidre ».

33. *In Lisieux, the church of Sainte-Thérèse (1929).*
34. *The capital of camembert cheese, Vimoutiers.*
35. *In the Pays d'Auge, apple trees along the « cider route ».*

36. L'abbaye aux Hommes à Caen, fondée en 1063.
37. Les remparts.
38. Notre-Dame de Livaye.

*36. The Abbaye aux Hommes, in Caen, founded in 1063.*
*37. The ramparts.*
*38. Notre-Dame de Livaye.*

37

38

39

40

41

39. Près de Caen, la château de la Fontaine Henry,
40. L'abbaye de Cerisy-la-Forêt fondée au VIᵉ siècle.
41. Sur la route des Moulins, l'église Saint-Pierre à Thaon.

*39. Near Caen, the chateau of Fontaine Henry.*
*40. The Abbaye of Cerisy-la-Forêt, founded in the VI century.*
*41. On the Moulins road, the St.-Pierre church, in Thaon.*

42

42. Les Britanniques et les Canadiens débarquèrent à Arromanches en juin 44.
*42. The British and Canadian troupes landed at Arromanche.*

43

43. On pêche la coquille Saint-Jacques à Port-en-Bessin.
*43. Sea scallops are fished at Port-en-Bessin.*

44

44. Notre-Dame de Bayeux, épargnée par la guerre.
45. Le château de Guillaume le Conquérant à Falaise.
46. Vendeuvre (vallée de la Dive), un château à la Mansart.

*44. Notre-Dame de Bayeux, undamaged by the war.*
*45. The chateau of Guillaume le Conquérant (William the Conqueror), in Falaise.*
*46. Vendeuvre (in the Dive valley), a chateau in the Mansart style.*

45

46

47

47. Entre l'Orne et la Sarthe, les Alpes Mancelles.
*47. Between the Orne and the Sarthe, the Mancelles Alpes.*

# ORNE,
# Green Normandy

The department of the Orne is the greenest in Normandy, where the industrial wave is less visible and served to revitalize the cities without affecting the « country » aspect of the region. The Regional Natural Park Normandie-Maine (234,000 hectares) covers a good quarter of the Orne. The park contains high clusters of oaks and forest beech trees from the forests of Ecouves and Andaines and is full of animals : deer, wild bores, foxes. It is also contains farm land criss-crossed by hedges and trees, which contributes to part of the economy of the Orne. The orchards of pear and apple trees were replanted several years ago and now flower beautifully in springtime.

## The Province of the Perche

The very old province of the Perche (1114) was divided into four departments during the Revolution of 1789, one of which was the Orne. The Perche is home to those large robust horses, brought, without a doubt, from the Arab countries by the Crusades. These horses pulled coaches and delivery wagons all the way to the streets of Paris. Motors replaced these large, handsome Percherons, but the Percheron Equestrian Society has kept genealogical records which go back to the beginning of the XIX century and to a fitting ancestor, « Jean Le Blanc ». If, on the road, one only rarely comes across these Percherons hitched up, they always participate in contests in the Perche.

Arriving in the Orne by the east, one enters directly into the historic decor of the department : Mortagne and Bellème, major cities in Norman Perche. In a hilly and wooded environment, the houses are constructed here with various material from the region-red sandstone, baked bricks, tiles-contrasting with the houses of the Auge region. In this region, to the north, wood panels and cobs are used. Around Mortagne, Bellème and all the way to the Aigle, a number of high quality manor-houses give an appearance of solidity, defying time and blending perfectly in the woods of Regional National Park of the Perche (182,000 hectares, classified January 16, 1998). Here, small departmental roads trace their way between the woods and the countryside.

Edging its « living and mysterious forest », as the writer Roger Martin du Gard described it, Bellème has long been at odds with Mortagne over which city is the capital of the Comté. This lively village owes its second wind to its being classed as a « green resort ». This fact attracts a number of tourists and hikers who are fond of « green tourism. » On the same plan as the old walled city of the XV century, one finds Medieval vestiges and hotels which once were the homes of the town notables in the XVIII century. Attractions not to be missed are : the Rue de la Ville Close, between the entry gate and the church, the Governor's house, the Bansard des Bois town house and other less noble, but none the less elegant, dwellings which surround the Saint-Sauveur church. The interior of the church offers brilliant surprises : lovely sculpting, superb baptisteries from the XVII century and a Transfiguration attributed to Oudry Sr.

Seventeen kilometers from there, is Mortagne-au-Perche, also fortified in the XV century. This place is a little rustic, well restored and full of flowers. A nice walk is between the Porte Saint-Denis and the Park which overlooks the hills of the Perche. Not to be missed is Notre-Dame church and its sumptuous wood-work from the XVIII century. At the Porte Saint-Denis, elevated to two floors in the XVI century, the Percheron Museum makes for an interesting visit. Just next door, the Hotel des Comtes de Perche, holds the memory of a certain Emile Chartier: the philosopher Alain, born here at number 3 Rue de la Comédie.

The Foire au Boudin (Sausage Fair) is an annual event which takes place during Lent. This onion-flavored sausage is made according to an ancestral tradition. An international tasting contest, arranged by the Confrérie du Goûte-Boudin, takes place and is topped off by an immense barbecue. (The sausages can also be found in the market on Saturdays.) In June and July the entire region attends the local horse races.

## The Countess's Market

To the north, on the road to Argentan, stands Aigle. During the War, Aigle lost the essential part of its elegant homes standing along the Risle. A fine example of industrial architecture of the XIX century, the Mérouvel factory is all that remains of major industry in Aigle from the XIX century, pins. In 1856, its famous animal market had its first sponsor, a Russian grande dame, Sophie Rostopchine, countess of Ségur. Forgotten by her too-charming husband, she stayed in the chateau of Nouettes, 4 kilometers away. She spent her time writing tales for children, stories which would make any teacher shudder. One of her stories « Memories of a Donkey » named Cadichon, took place in the Aigle market.

This market, third largest in France, every Tuesday, brings together a crowd of curious and serious spectators. Around the market one finds the settings used for her stories: the Risle valley, the Saint-Evroult forest, the pin factory. The chateau de Ségur is occupied by a Medico-Pedagogical Institute, but in the church residence of Aube-sur-Risle, souvenirs, portraits, small pieces of furniture and dolls dressed in period costumes are on display, as proper young ladies, of course.

## Lace from Alençon

In the agricultural plain in the south of the Orne, Alençon was the capital of needle lace until the end of the last century. The city furnished inestimable bridal veils to all the courts of Europe. During the time of Louis XIV, eight thousand young women worked to make this lace, a refined version of Venice lace. In 1665, Colbert created a law for the Gobelins tapestry factory and at the same time a Royal Lace Factory for this « French stitched » lace and forbade the importation of any foreign lace. Until 1950 this tedious work was continued. It took four hours of work to make one square centimeter of lace, using only a needle and thread as fine as a hair for tools. To preserve the secret of its fabrication, each worker was taught a single lace design for the finished work, one design and one only.

Mechanical lace making has replaced the Alençon stitch as well as that of other laces. If the lace school of the National Workshop of Alençon continues to teach this ancient craft, it is not because lace makes the town's fortune. It is rather household appliances. In 1937, Mr. Mantelet decentralized his vegetable mill factory, before this practice became generalized. His product was enjoying a certain amount of success at this time. Then the products became equipped with electric motors. Today twelve appliance factories contribute to the economy of Lower-Normandy.

In the very lovely Medieval Lamagdelaine Square, the Gothic church of Notre-Dame and the Ozé House (Tourist Office) are in the center of a large pedestrian area. This area takes in most of the Grande Rue and the pretty Clémenceau Court. The houses (classed as historical monuments) have hardly changed since the time of Balzac and make *La Vieille Fille* (The Old Maid) come alive. Today, lively with boutiques, this is the place where everyone in Alençon passes through. The new University Center, which groups schools of technology and industry, has today attracted modern young people. From Notre-Dame, by way of the Rue aux Sieurs, one arrives at the Grand Hall of Wheat, the former agricultural market. It is a fine example of metal architecture of the XIX century. One arrives at the chateau, as well, now a gigantic ruin whose crowned tower gives some indication of what Alençon must have been during the Middle Ages.

A visit to the capital of the Orne would not be complete without at least three museums. At the Museum of Fine Art, there are collections of lace from every workshop in the world: Chantilly, Malines, Brussels, Venice...as well as a rare collection of paintings, thanks to the marquis of Chennevière, a citizen of Alençon and an astute collector. The marquis was Director of Fine Art under Napoleon III. He took advantage of his position to decorate his home town museum with exceptional works by French, Italian and Flemish painters of the XVII century. Included also are canvases by Courbet, Boudin, and Fantin-Latour. The Conservatory Museum for Alençon Lace is housed in what was the headquarters of General Leclerc. On the ground floor one can see objects and films explaining the delicate manufacture of lace, while on the upper floor one finds documents, trophies and souvenirs retracing the campaign of the 2nd Armored Division which liberated the city on August 12, 1944. At number 50 of the Rue Saint-Blaise, finally, a bourgeois house from the last century where the daughter of a clock maker and a lace worker was born in 1873. Her name was Thérèse Martin, the future Sainte-Thérèse. The house is now a museum in her memory.

## The Mancelles Alps

Leaving Alençon, one only has to leave the road to Rennes to cross the Mancelles Alps. Alps is a curious name for this fresh stream-crossed region, whose highest summit, Mount-des-Avaloirs, rises only to 417 meters, the lowest point in the Normandy-Maine Park along with the Signal des Ecouves. One does have, however, a superb view over the forest. Hardly 14 kilometers from there, in a bend in the Sarthe, the village of Saint-Cénery-le-Gérei with its stone houses, seems forgotten by time. With its small low houses and its touching Romanesque church, it is one of the most beautiful villages in France. On the Sarthe, the little old bridge under the willow trees gives one a moment of pure poetry.

Between Alençon and Carrouges, the Ecouves Forest covers some 150,000 hectares. It was designed under the reign of Louis XIV, with large passages arranged like the points of a star around elegant round-abouts, it is the traditional meeting place for huntsmen. At the entry to the Normandy-Maine Park, the chateau of Carrouges (like the chateau d'O near Argentan) is an astonishing example of secular Gothic construction. From the little entry chateau, surrounded by trees, the high slate roofs of the chateau, punctuated by towers made of small pink bricks, criss-crossed with brown, enchants the visitor. The interior of the chateau has been renovated to the decor of Louis XIII or Louis XVI, according to furnished rooms and bedrooms. Even the kitchen displays a collection of shining copper utensils and object from another epoch, enough to make magazines envious. In the buildings of the former chapel, the Maison du Parc, distributes information and maps for hiking.

# Bagnoles de l'Orne, Horse Springs

Around the lake formed by the Vée, Bagnoles-de-l'Orne has kept its Belle Epoque atmosphere thanks to the lovely houses from the last century.

Legend has it that a house discovered the spring which furnishes water for Bagnoles. In the Middle Ages, the Knight Hugues de Tessé abandoned his aging mount in the forest. A month later the horse came back to the stable so frisky that the knight, believing what was good for the horse must be good for the man as well, tried this miraculous spring himself. His success was convincing. People continue to use the water from Bagnoles for health and medicinal purposes. In 1691, a certain Dr. Legeay from Alençon, more astute, created three swimming pools, one for men, one for women (both of which charged a fee) and one for the poor which was free. At the beginning of the Second Empire, the waters at Bagnoles were used but in rather primitive conditions. In 1869, the arrival of the railroad brought with it the duke of Morny, Dumas, the count Waleswski and Barbey d'Aurevilly, which made the resort quite fashionable. In 1880, the company « La Foncière de France » constructed the Grand Hotel des Thermes and a casino, which made « high society » possible for the area. In 1886, the Foncière bought 45 hectares of land on the lake, designed the lovely boulevards that we know today, and sold lots. The villas date from this time. The houses had to be built of red sandstone and wood, with towers, bay windows, ridge pole roofing, etc. In the park designed for promenades, an elegant Thermal Bath was built. It is still there. Bagnoles, with its waters at 25° C. is today the first thermal resort in France for the treatment of venous afflictions and has now found a young clientele with its fitness programs and pure air which has proved to be a remarkable sedative. Dating from the last century, the Grand Hotel rents its terraced rooms overlooking the lake as apartments, as do most of the large 1900 villas. Around the little train station, some were torn down in favor of more modern constructions. Enough villas still remain, however, to provide a pretty itinerary through the Belle Époque.

Part of the houses from the golden age stand on the hills of Tessé-la-Madeleine, around the chateau of the Madeleine (called Roches-Bagnoles) which serves as town hall for this charming commune. From the Roc du Chien (Dog Rock), to the right of the chateau, one has a perfect view overlooking Bagnoles and its lake.

In the Andaines Forest, which surrounds Bagnoles-de-l'Orne, 7,000 hectares of trees and 14 centuries of legends, including that of Lancelot of the Lake, await visitors at the Ermitage d'Ortaire, on Mount Charlemagne. Two-hundred and fifty kilometers of hiking trails, easy and well-marked, to follow on foot, by bicycle, on horseback or even in a horse drawn carriage, with itineraries, and perhaps a guide or a coach driver make this a hiker's paradise.

## The Chateau of Aliénor

At Domfront, the dungeon of the enormous chateau has kept watch over the Varenne for eight centuries. One of the strongest chateau-fortresses of the XII century, it was one of the favorite residences of Aliénor of Aquitaine and Henri II, who held a brilliant court here. It is believed that Chrétien-de-Troyes was inspired by Domfront for his legend of Lancelot of the Lake. Archeological research carried out since 1982 have uncovered vestiges of very large priory of Saint-Symphorien, dating from 1010.

The streets of the Medieval city-old cobblestones and half-timbered houses-are squeezed within the fortifications of which thirteen towers still exist from the twenty-four original ones. A local specialty is poiré (perry), made in the traditional way. This became so rare that the villages of the region have replanted hectares of white pear trees. One can still find poiré in the Saturday market or at the local fairs (first and second Mondays of the month). One can also find Calvados from Domfront, with it's very particular taste: they add pears.

Continuing towards Argentan, Sée is worth a stop if only for its cathedral, a masterpiece of Norman Gothic art. The facade may have lost a little of its elegance because of the supports which reinforce the porch, but the nave, the transept and the XIII century windows all make an admirable frame for the marble altar, signed Brousseau. During the summer, evening concerts and light shows add to the elegance of the stones.

## The Argentan Region

At the crossroads of a major highway and an important railway line, on the road of the Liberation, Argentan was 90% destroyed during the Avranche campaign on August 7, 1944. It was a hard battle as a marked tour illustrates. This lovely little town, somewhat neglected at the end of the war, has seen its economy reactivated by nearby food-product industries which have tripled its 1944 population.

Argentan is a bit better because of having discovered needle lace well before Alençon, as its origin goes back to 1378. Benedictine nuns (from an abbey with a steeple) perpetuate the tradition and still make this meticulous embroidery in their workshop. Next to the abbey, a recent House of Argentan Lace displays fairy tale collection. Courses in lace making are offered. Something to remember: it takes six to seven years to train a lace maker.

A horse breeding center, the Argentan region is also the country of chateaux, certain ones of which may be visited. Sassy, Medavy and, on the Sées road, the chateau d'O are names to be remembered. Reflected in its pond, the chateau d'O is an astonishing flamboyant Gothic building whose towers frame an entry of a very complex architectural style. Patiently restored and re-furnished, O possesses two Renaissance pigeon houses as lovely as chateaux.

## Colbert's Horses

At Le Pin, the existence of a royal stud farm of fifty-six horses goes back to Philippe VI, at the beginning of the Hundred Years War. But it was Colbert, « inventor » of the royal stud farm, who, in 1715, ordered the construction of the Le Pin Stud Farm. The construction took fifteen years. The elegant stone and pale brick buildings, set high on a wooded hill, in gardens strictly designed by Le Nôtre, admirably justify the nickname of « The Versailles of Horses ». The construction of this Royal Stud Farm incited private stud farms to develop in the neighborhood. These farms today raise over half of all French purebred horses. The Le Pin Stud Farm trains technicians, grooms and blacksmiths. Stallions, French and English trotters, Percherons and purebreds are raised here. The presentation of harnessing, mounted stallions and equestrian contests of the Farm attract numerous adepts from everywhere. The collection of carriages, saddles and workshops, as well as the gardens are open for visits.

## The Home of the Camembert

In the north of the Orne, the decor changes. Small green and cool valleys, apple orchards, houses made of crude plaster and wooden panels, farms where the principal activity revolves around dairy products: we are in the Auge Region (Pays d'Auge) which continues into the department of Calvados. The most famous cheese of Normandy was invented here during the Revolution, in the village of Camembert, which gave the cheese its name. Marie Harel, a farm woman at the chateau de Beaumoncel, found the recipe. Her statue stands in the village, a gift from an industrial cheese factory in Ohio. One cannot visit the Beaumoncel manor, but the local tourist office had the good idea to set up a House of Camembert in the village. With its creamery and two farms, the village still makes the cheese in the traditional method.

Finally, in Vimoutiers, in the Camembert Museum, antique wooden and copper utensils reconstruct a creamery of the last century and a prodigious collection of cheese labels remind us of the Auge Region's vocation for two centuries. The reputation of this cheese, its quality due to raw milk, exclusively from Normandy and hand molded with a ladle (A.O.C. 1983), has crossed oceans. In America, Japan and Australia, « camembert » is manufactured, alas, with pasteurized milk!

## The Priory

Between Camembert and Vimoutiers, the Saint-Michel Priory, in Crouttes, is something to see. In a priory of the XIII century, where a « modest community » of Benedictines once lived, stand a barn sagging under its heavy beams, a Romanesque chapel, one of the oldest cider presses in Normandy (XV century), its cellar (XIV century), a bakery and a dwelling for priors (XVIII century). A massive and superb collection, restored stone by stone by private persons in love with the site. A permanent (and changing) Edgar Chahine exposition and a display of paintings, photographs and sculptures give life to this special place. Twenty-four hectares of gardens surround it: simple gardens in the monastic tradition where forgotten vegetables and rose bushes dating from years past add their poetry to this old priory.

48. L'église romane de Saint-Céneri-le-Gerei.
*48. On the Sarthe River, the Romanesque church of Saint-Céneri-le-Gérei.*

49

49. Le petit pont roman de Saint-Céneri-le-Gerei (Orne).
50. Au bord de l'Orne, Sées, un évêché dès le IVᵉ siècle.

49. *The little Romanesque bridge of Saint-Céneri-le-Gérei (Orne river).*
50. *On the banks of the Orne, Sées, a bishop's palace from the IV century.*

51

52

51. Dans l'Orne, on élève des chevaux depuis cinq siècles.

*51. Horses have been raised in the Orne region for five centuries.*

52. Le Haras du Pin : haras royal construit pour Louis XIV.

52. *The Haras du Pin : a royal stud farm built for Louis XIV.*

53. Le château d'O,
une petite merveille
Renaissance.

*53. The chateau d'O,
a small gem from
the Renaissance.*

53

54

55

56

54. Dominant Bagnoles-de-l'Orne, Tessé-la-Madeleine.
55. Le donjon à machicoulis du château de Gacé dans l'Orne.
56. À Carrouges, on peut visiter le château de briques rouges.

*54. Overlooking Bagnoles from the Orne, Tessé-la-Madeleine.*
*55. The machicolated dungeon of the chateau of Gacé, in the Orne region.*
*56. At Carrouges, the red brick chateau may be visited.*

57

57. Le lac de Bagnoles-de-l'Orne et l'ex-Grand Hôtel (1880).

57. *The lake of Bagnoles de l'Orne and the former Grand Hotel (1880).*

58

58. Saint-Léonard-des-Bois.

58. *Saint-Léonard-des-Bois* .

59. Point de vue
imprenable sur la
Vire depuis les
roches de Ham.

59. *The Ham rocks,*
*an unrestricted view*
*over the Vire river.*

60. Près de La Hague, Ormonville-la-Rogue.

60. *Near the Hague, Ormonville-la-Rogue.*

61

61. L'abbaye de Hambye dans la vallée de la Sienne.

*61. The Abbaye de Hambye, in the Sienne valley.*

62. Courbet peignit la Grande Cascade de Mortain.

*62. Coubet painted the « Grande Cascade de Mortain » (the Mortain waterfalls).*

# THE MANCHE,
## Between the Sea and Farmland

Three-hundred and thirty kilometers of coastline, eight marinas, nine lighthouses are all part of the Manche ; full of history, from the Norman invaders to the English. A department with two faces and two types of economy. Along the coast lies the Contentin, the ocean side and the end of land. This is the most preserved coastline in France, 3000 hectares to protect the Bay of Les Veys, Utah-Beach, Tatihou, La Hague Le Nez de Jobourg, and of course Le Mont. Fishing, maritime traffic, sailing and tourism are all important. On the land side, there is the Regional Natural Park of the Cotentin-Bessin. The park consists of 1150,000 hectares of farmland criss-crossed by hedges and trees and stretches from the Bay of Les Veys to the east to Le Harve and from Saint-Germain-sur-Ay in the west all the way to north of Saint-Lô. This is a department for dairy and vegetable farms and a paradise for hunters of water fowl, green tourism and abbeys.

## On the Land Side, Saint Lô

A bishopric since the VI century and fortified by Charlemagne, Saint-Lô was so destroyed in 1944 that it is called the « capital of ruins. » The Americans arrived there after the « hell of the hedges, » a hard campaign, involving foot soldiers in terrible combats across deep routes, high embankments, and farmland. A key crossroads for the German army as well as for the Allies, crushed by bombs from June 6, the city was recaptured after hand-to-hand combat one street at a time. On July 19, nothing was left of the old part of Saint-Lô but the shattered towers of the collegiate church of Notre-Dame and several houses in the suburbs-but the city was finally liberated.

From the ruins has risen a modern and active city. An administrative capital since the Empire, its location in an agricultural region makes it a seat for mutual benefit societies, cooperatives, and schools (I.U.T., business school and hotel management school). A regional showcase, the Saturday market in General-de-Gaulle square is pure pleasure. Merchants coming from farms and the coast offer shell fish, live seafood, the day's catch of fish as well as mouth-watering farm cheeses, and fruit picked that very morning, Small farmers come to the market sea. Another is the town of Ys, the Middle Age port sinking in the waves. As a matter of perspective, the church on its promontory is in the center of the town. Protected by Saire point, Saint Vaast-la-Hougue has only triumphant memories. It was here that in 1346, Edward III of England debarked to bring the Hundred Years War to France. It was here that the French fleet was defeated by the English fleet in 1692. History has its revenge, as Saint-Vaast was the first port liberated on the morning of June 6, 1944. A fishing port and pleasure port with well protected sandy beaches, it has become a peaceful seaside resort.

The small island of Tatihou, so close to Saint-Vaast that one can walk to it with dry feet during low tide, is a bird sanctuary. Its particularity, its Vauban fort, contains an astonishing museum : wrecked ships of all sorts, weapons, everyday objects, all recovered from boats sunk in 1692 in La Hougue.

## Utah Beach, On That Day...

From Quineville to the Bay of Les Veys, without thinking one follows the beaches and dunes of Varreville. The coastal road, however, is called the « road of the Allies ». Utah Beach is here! In bad weather, in the foggy dawn, one imagines the debarkation ships, men jumping into the cold water and the blockhouses spitting out death. It was June 6, 1944.

Five miles further back, Sainte-Mère-Eglise is today, along with Isigny (Calvados), the cream and butter capital. An agricultural burg with its pastures, it is a village like so many others which entered into history that day at 2:00 o'clock in the morning when American parachutists literally fell upon it. Their mission was to clear the exits of Utah Beach. Next to the farm from the XVI century where furniture, tools, and objects reconstruct everyday farm life, Sainte-Mère now has a museum of the airborne troops. In front of the town hall, a large cement marker stands on kilometer 00 of the Road to Liberty.

Closing Utah Beach, the Bay of Les Veys is included in the zone protected by the Cotentin and Bessin Regional Natural Park. At the end of the long pass which joins it with the sea, Carentan is literally « at sea level » : during high tide it is only 1.5 meters above sea level. Its location between Utah Beach and Omaha Beach made it a likely victim in 1944. Almost spared by the war, the Notre-Dame church, the arcades around Republic Square, the very old Fontaines public laundry and the town hall make it a refreshing stop. Since 1982, a dug marina offers more secure mooring. Thus, Carentan, having become an enormous agricultural market for transit goods, has once again found its place as capital of the country of cream.

63

63. Sainte-Mère-Église, la première ville libérée en juin 44.
*63. Sainte-Mère-Église, the first town to be liberated.*

69.

70.

69. À un kilomètre de La Hougue, l'ilet de Tatihou.
70. À Tatihou, un petit fort-musée et des parcs à huîtres.

69. One kilometer from La Hougue lies the islet of Tatihou.
70. In Tatihou, a small museum fort and oyster beds.

73

73. Bien abritée par La Hague, l'anse Saint-Martin.

*73. Well sheltered by La Hague, Saint-Martin Cove.*

74

74. Le village de Gatteville.

74. *The village of Gatteville.*

75. Port Lévy.

*75. Port Lévy*

76

76. Le port de Cherbourg, reconstruit après la guerre.
77. Côté « Vieux Cabourg », le quai Alexandre III.
78. Au raz de la Hague, le minuscule port Racine.

76. *The port of Cherbourg, reconstructed after the war.*
77. *A bit of « Old Cherbourg », the quay Alexander III.*
78. *Near La Hague, the minuscule Port Racine.*

77

78

79

80

79. Sur un chemin de douaniers, Omonville-la-Rogue.
80. Le phare de La Hague, le « Finistère » normand.

*79. On the Customs road, Omonville-la-Rogue.*
*80. The La Hague lighthouse, the « lands-end » of Normandy.*

# CALVADOS,
## Historical Beaches

This is a department whose vocation is tourism. There is everything here for the tourist. Some 200 kilometers from Paris, the fine sandy beaches, which were already charming painters and writers during the last century, have become resorts with a charm of yesteryear with their golf courses, casinos, racetracks and hotels of all categories. Add gastronomy, sea food and dairy products to all this and you have a center for « Norman cuisine ». A stone's throw from the coast, one finds the historic cities whose decor is known throughout the world. The Bocage and the Pays d'Auge possess villages seem to have been lifted directly from a post card. Actually it is not the apple alcohol which gives Calvados its name, but rather the Revolution. In 1789, the deputies were looking for departmental names which had nothing to do with the Old Regime. The Norman Delauney came up with « Calvados », the name of a rock that is uncovered only at very high tides.

### From Omaha Beach to Bayeux

Polders have made the mud flats of the wide Bay of Les Veys into fine agricultural lands, included in the Cotentin-Bessin Park. It is a sanctuary for birds, curlews, ducks and dotterels. After the war, Isigny-sur-Mer, at the back of the bay, hardly had anything left but its lovely Louis XVI town hall. Isigny, today, along with Sainte-Mère, is known for its dairy products which were already renowned in the XVII century. At the entrance to the bay, the Pointe du Hoc was one of the crucial points for the Allied Debarkation. From this height (30 meters), a German battalion sprayed the beaches with bullets. They had to be crushed with bombs and shells before a murderous assault. A granite peak and shattered earth bear witness that Omaha Beach began there.

Not too enthusiastic about the place, but fascinated by a sea so different from his Mediterranean, Emile Zola was astonished at the « army of chalets » which were constructed around the port in Bessin. This pretty port, protected by its stone jetties, is identical to that which was painted by Seurat in 1879. Fishermen bring fish and sea scallops from trawlers. The marina (which is always full in summer) and the terraces create an atmosphere that is as it must have been before the war. A memory? « The Town Hall of the Port » (*La Marie du Port*), a film with Jean Gabin.

tury, in a splendid checkerboard of stones and varnished bricks; the dungeon is topped with tiles with its sharp towers, stands against the half timbered original building. Frescos and very beautiful furnishings add elegance. Very near, Orbec is the most poetic burg in all Normandy. From pretty Renaissance half-timbered houses bordering the Rue Grande (where Debussy composed the poetic « Gardens in the Rain ») to the church of the same epoch, it is a pure delight. The manor is elegant with its sculpted XVI timbers and houses the municipal museum, which is well worth a visit. Not in keeping with its name, this little museum presents a charming mixture of popular traditional arts, historical documents and paintings.

## Pilgrimage to Lisieux

In the Touques valley, Lisieux is today the most important commercial center in the Auge Region. The city has been prominent in the history of Normandy since the Gaulois epoch, but it is for a small Carmelite who died at the age of 24, Sainte Thérèse de l'Enfant Jésus, that thousands of pilgrims come here every year. The memories of the little nun, canonized in 1925, require a long stroll. This cloister, where she entered at the age of 15 years and 3 months, with a dispensation from the pope, displays her marble recumbent statue and memories. On the road to Trouville, one may visit the Buissonnets, the « charming house with a belvedere and a view which stretches far » where she lived when she was 4. The gardens are the same as she liked them. The « bedroom of the miracle » where, at the age of 10, she was visited by the Virgin, has been reconstituted and displays her communion dress and toys. At the other end of Lisieux, on the road to Orbec, the immense basilica Sainte-Thérèse, built in 1954, covering 4,500 square meters, has the merit of being the largest church built in the XX century and is signed by a number of people: Robert Coin, Pierre Gaudin.

Historical Lisieux also exists. In the Public Garden, the former Bishop's Garden, Saint-Pierre cathedral (1170-1260) is beautifully simple with a pure flamboyant Gothic chapel. Next to it, the Palais de Justice (Court House) is installed in the Episcopal Palace of the XIII century. Several streets still lined with Norman houses, lead to the Museum of Old Lisieux. Housed in a pleasant half timbered dwelling, an agreeable mix of documents about Lisieux and the Auge region, traditional popular art objects, earthenware, jewels, furniture and statues are on display.

1

_81

81. L'heure du « rayon vert » sur la Manche.

81. *The time of « green rays » on the Channel.*

82

82. Le Nez de Jobourg, au pied des falaises.
83. La baie d'Escalgrain, plages entre les falaises.
84. De longues dunes à Escalgrain.
85. Des plages sans fin : la côte ouest du Cotentin

82. *The Nez de Jobourg, at the foot of the cliffs.*
83. *The bay of Escalgrain, beaches between the cliffs.*
84. *Long sand dunes as well, at Escalgrain.*
85. *Endless beaches : the western coast of Cotentin.*

83

84

90

91

92

90. La remarquable cathédrale de Coutances.
91. Un jardin avec panorama à Coutances.
92. Le château de Pirou, l'un des plus anciens de Normandie.

90. *The remarkable cathedral of Coutances.*
91. *A garden with a panoramic view, in Coutances.*
92. *The chateau of Pirou, one of the oldest in Normandy.*

93

94

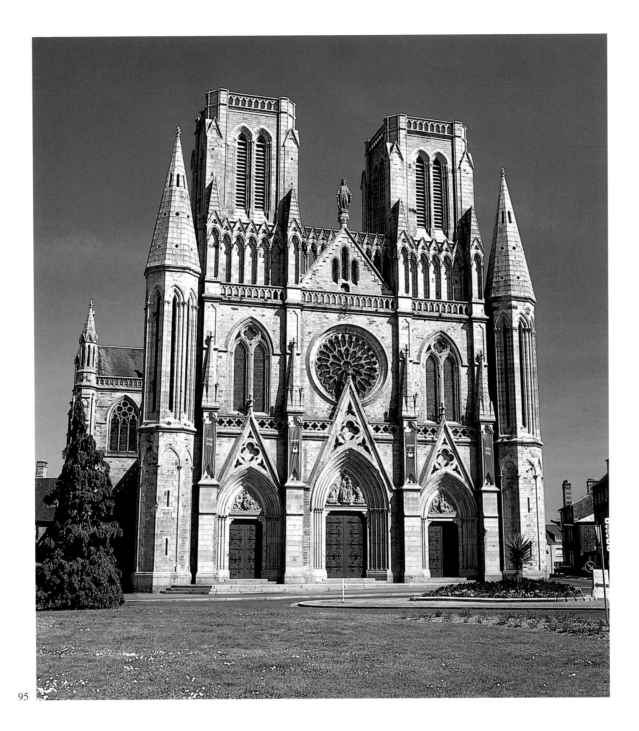

95

93. À Granville, la Ville Close domine le port.
94. Plaisance et parcs à huîtres à Granville.
95. Près d'Avranches, Notre-Dame-des-Champs.
96. Le Mont-Saint-Michel... dès la fin du XIIᵉ siècle.

93. *In Granville, the walled city overlooks the port.*
94. *Pleasure boats and oyster beds : Granville.*
95. *Near Avranches, Notre-Dame-des-Champs.*
96. *The Mont-Saint-Michel ... from around the end of the XII century.*

96 ▶

97. La « Merveille » à la haute mer du soir.
*97. The « Merveille » (Miracle), at high tide in the evening.*

# THE ROAD TO FREEDOM

The road of the Debarkation and the Battle of Normandy constitute an itinerary which is still inseparable from the five Norman departments. It begins on the beaches of the Manche and Calvados and continues over 72 kilometers. But in fact, the Road to Freedom goes all the way to Bastogne, in Belgium, there, where Patton's tanks definitively stopped the German offensive.

On June 6, 1944, quiet seaside resorts called Crisbecq, Sainte-Marie du Mont, Port en Bessin, Arromanches, Ouistreham...took on their war names: Utah Beach, Omaha Beach, Gold, Juno, Sword. The road of memories begins at the Place de la République, in Sainte-Mère-Eglise, where the airborne troops jumped on the night of June 6. They prepared Operation Overlord: the Debarkation. On the square, a large granite monument marks kilometer 00 of the «Road to Liberty» and these markers dot the route all the way to Bastogne.

This same June 6, between 6:30 and 7:55 o'clock, in rather cloudy weather, the boats fought waves of over 2 meters high and threw men on beaches which were mined and defended by batteries of blockhouses. Utah Beach, from Saint-Vaast to the Carentan canal formed the eastern face of the Cotentin (Manche); Omaha Beach, Gold, Juno and Sword,

from Pointe du Hoc to Ouistreham formed the Calvados coast. At 8:00 pm, the liaison between Carentan, Bayeux and Caen was established. A bloody day was finished but hard battles were yet to come. Eventually, though, seven years of nightmares came to an end.

The figures: This one day of June 6, 1944 required 6900 ships, 11,590 airplanes, 20,000 vehicles and 484, 621 men, of which 156,700 were paratroopers. The day cost 10,00 lives. From Day J to August 29 in Paris, more than 2 million men participated in the Battle of Normandy. To relate a little story, for their progression from the Normandy coasts to Paris, the allied troops had only Michelin maps from 1939...from the Red Guide. They used these for maps of the cities. On the Road to Freedom, sixteen museums on the beaches and in Norman cities keep the memories of the stages of these battlee as well as 27 cemeteries (of which 16 are British) where English, American and Canadian families of those soldiers who gave their lives come to pay their respects. There are German german graves, because more than 50,000 tombs of German soldiers are in Normandy. (Itineraries are in the C.D.T. of the Manche, Calvados and all Norman cities and the authentic Michelin map of the Debarkation has been re-edited).

153

# ITINERARIES IN NORMANDY

For more specific discoveries, the Normandy departements have put together attractive itineraries baste on specific themes, from 40 to 100 kilometers, easily followed during a week-end. They include useful addresses, interesting stopovers and often gastronomic suggestions.

## SEINE MARITIME

### The Garden Road.

With the climate helping, gardens are a fine art in the Seine Maritime, some of them are masterpieces. The star of gardens is the Parc du Bois de Moutiers, created a century ago by the English architect Luytens. More than 10 hectares of sophisticated gardens and a fabulous collection of azalias, rhododendrams and camelias await the visitor. At the chateau Miromesnil, in Tourville-sur-Arques, flowerbeds of cabbage and herbs compose strict decorations. The gardens of Bosmelet, around a Louis XIII chatear, are worthy of the King's Vegetable Garden, the same may be said for the gardens of the Galleville chateau, near Doudeauville. There are also the exotic collections of Bellevue in Beaumont-le-Hareng. At Saint-Valéry-en-Caux, a lovely garden of « weeds, mixes wild camomile, neetles, bindweed and many other medicinal plants. » In Montmain, near Rouen, finally, the Jardin d'Angélique was composed by her parents to the memory of a departed young girl who dreamed of a fairy garden. Old fashioned roses clime old apple trees and arbors with their pastel flowers. It is the garden of which Angélique dreamed.

### The Dovecote Road

Fifty-five kilometers long, through the valleys of the Durdent and Valmont de Ganzeville, will take one to see fifteen exceptional dovecotes, their roffs shaped like a pepper-grinder, a symbol of the authority of the lords of the manors. Along this route of dovecotes, one finds the clos-masures of the Caux Region and the Dovecote Museum in Oharville, on the grounds of the Auffray Manor.

### The Apple and Cider Road

For devotees of regional products, from Auffray to Longueville-sur-Scie, there are 38 kilometers of well-marked roads between orchards and cider producers. Included are addresses of fruit farms selling apples and cider.

## And Even More

Forty-eight rare small churches in the Seine-Maritime department, well indicated ; the Ivory and Spice rout, between Dieppe and Fécamp; the Route of Glass, through the valley of the Bresle, from Aumale to Mers-les-Bains, where some 15 million perfume bottles are manufactured for famous brands, among others (maps and information available from the tourist office in Rouen).

# EURE

The Eure along the Water and Norman Vexin, at the border of the Ile de France, from Gisors, Verneuil-sur-Avre, makes up a tour of 90 kilometers, all the way to Evreux. One finds chateaux in the Ouches region, Breteuil-sur-Iton, Francheville.

## The Cottage Route

These « humble dwellings » crowned with straw and flowers are carefully kept up today. Some fifty kilometers, between the Seine and Forests, winds from Brotonne to Marais Vernier going through villages that are more Norman than nature: Vieux-Pont, near the Seine, Aizier, Sainte-Opportune-la-Mare.

## The Seine by Bicycle

Maurice Leblanc followed this itinerary, 25 kilometers over the roads of the Regional Natural Park of Brotonne, with stops in ten rural museums, the Forge museum, the Linin Museum, the Bread Museum... and the Marais Vernier. Or one can go by car...through the Seine of pastel colors. This tour takes three days on roads which the painters followed, gastronomic discoveries included.

## The Railway of the Valley of the Eure

From Pacy-sur-Eure to Breuilpont, this zigzags by roads and highways through villages and tiny burgs.

And Even More : Follow the road of the 7th Art and discover settings where films were made; there is the route of Mills. Updated each year, the Eure in summer is an invitation to coolness and exceptional visits (all addresses at the tourist office in Evreux).

# ORNE

## The Stud Farm and Chateau Road

Fifty to 185 kilometers ; for an itinerary of the most spectacular locations in the department. The Haras du Pin, the private chateaux (including O and Medavy), the museum chateau of Flers, Carrouges, the Sées cathedral, the churches of Saint-Germain d'Argentan, Notre Dame-sur-l'Eau in Domfront, the Abbatiale de Lonlay-l'Abbaye, the Ferté-Macé. In the same style, the « Route of Parks and Gardens » goes from Monceau, in the Perche, to Prieuré Saint-Pierre in Crouttes, passing through Sées, Argentan, Le Pin, Vimoutiers, etc.

## The Three Forests Road

For nature lovers, from Mêle-sur-Sarthe to Domfronnnt, 60 kilometers through protected forests of Ventes de Bourses, Ecouves and Andaines; historical sites, Bagnoles de l'Orne... Or even more, « Perch, Forests and Abbeys » at 150 kilometers from Paris, a small tour around Mortagne, for woods and great monuments

## Swiss Normandy

To the north-east of the Orne, 60 kilometers over the most « visual » part of the Orne Valley, from Argentan to Condé-sur-Noireau ; and still more : the Marguerite of Lorraine Tour, dutchess of Alençon, who watched over restoration in the region after the Hunddred Years War ; chateaux, maonoor, religious orders, a fine and intelligent tour. The Lancelot du Lac, poetic tour, around the Andaines. Of course, a « Lace Tour » from Alençon to Argentann (maps and addresses from the tourist office in Alençon).

# MANCHE

## The Abbey and Priory Road.

A magic tour, along the Cotentin, Mortain to Mont-Saint-Michelllll all the way to Cherbourg, passing by major sites of the department : Hambye, Coutances, Lessay, Bricquebec, Valognes, Carentan, Cerisy and the capital cities.

## The Touristic Train of the Cotentin

This train runs from Carteret to Port-Bail, along the coast of the islands. It crosses wild plains, dunes and bocage and passes by Carteret and its three churches : Saint-Jean, Saint-Georges-de-la-Rivière and Portbail, a village full of history. There is a bar and entertainment on bord the train.

## Paths Along the Coast

Great for hiking or short storlls between the sea and the land. From Mong-Saint-Michel to the Val-de-Saire, 230 kilometers of well-marked roads cross dunes and villages, run along the cliffs and go around the lighthouses.

## Towpaths

Along the Vire, the roads where men and horses pulled barges have been re worked and are now accessible for walking, horseback riding or cycling. Along the way one passes the locks, fish ladders... by rail which crosses the southern part of the Manche from one side to the other. It passes by forgotten countrysides with stops in Sourdeval, Pontaubault, Barenton, Saint-Hilaire-du-Harcouët. Converted into a hiking trail, it is a timeless walk.

## Bicycle Routes

For easy bicycle riding in this flat country, well-marked itineraries cross major sites using very small roads. Already in place, the Bay of Sienne, the Valley of the Vire, the Marais Park. Caution : a car may also be used... with prudence.

# CALVADOS

## The Route of the Mills

From Caen to Bayeux, from Thaon, the tour of villages in the region (Rucqueville, Saint-Gabriel, Amblie, Lantheuil), around charming Romanesque churches. Chateaux (for example, Creully, Fontaine-Henry) complete this lovely circuit...but there are very few mills!

## The Cheese Road

South of Trouville, along the Touques, of course passing by Pont l'Evêque and Livarot, but also Fervaques, Saint-Michel-du-Livet, Notre-Dame-de-Courson and especially Lisores, for a visit to the farm museum of Fernand Léger and his canvases, a giant mosaic and painted glass windows in the little chapel.

## The Cider Road

To the north of the Auge Region, this small tour is best done in the spring, when the apple trees are in bloom. From Caen or the Floral Coast, one goes to Cambremer, Beuvron, l'Abbaye de Val-Richer, the Victot chateau, Saint-Denis, with « practical » stops at cider producers and markets.

## The Marais Road

This leaves from Dives-sur-Mer (D.513). Around the Dives, the Middle Age salt flats, now damp prairies, are bordered by willow and poplar trees as well as aquatic flowers. Along little roads that zigzag, one comes upon villages, churches, abbeys, at Trooarn, Criqueville-en-Auge....

## And Still More

The Floral Coast, between Saint-Pierre-sur-Dives and the estuary of the Seine (Honfleur), there are admirable beaches, sharp cliffs, each one different and seaside resorts which take one back to the Belle Epoque (information at the Calvados tourist office in Caen).